CH00829680

The Lost

Sarah Gordon's precise and beautifully austere poems bear witness to a consciousness honed to confront humanity's most intriguing and vital questions. *The Lost Thing* is about love and loss, remorse, devotion, and retrieval. The poems disclose secrets and mysteries, especially in matters of "memory's fierce embrace." Although aware of the dangers of "rushing forward into the light," Gordon interrogates words, silences, and gestures. She can be as startling as Dickinson and as adroit as Moore with her acerbic observations. Despite her reserve, she finds forbidden beauty and elation in her personal remembrances of things past, and her "The Elysian Café" even foresees a forgiving afterlife. She "snags the heart," yet never disengages her extraordinary mind in these wonderful gifts to readers.

—R.T. Smith, author of *Summoning Shades*

In her new collection, Sarah Gordon shows herself to be a master of delicate subtlety, of poems that "disclose / this, just this much, / and no more." Poems that look for— often through the eyes of the remembered child—the "lost thing," hoping for yet fearing its inevitable resurrection. These are cool-eyed poems with hints of roiling underneath; that she maintains that balance is proof of her control and talent. A great read.

—Alice Friman, author of *Blood Weather*

With the light of her exacting and redemptive intelligence, Sarah Gordon celebrates the past and present history of a life well-lived and examined. Even the lost thing of the book's title poem reveals the emotional dimensions of its loss almost as if it had been found. The uniqueness of identity and the inherent value of experience are rediscovered over and over. *The Lost Thing* is a book of loving retrievals.

—Mark Jarman, author of *The Heronry*

Sarah Gordon's poems in *The Lost Thing* constitute a poetry of witness—yet rather than witness to the grand events of an era they offer a witness to the local events of a life, long and lovingly lived. These are poems that chronicle the poet's losses, yet they almost immediately become our own, particularly the loss of the unnamed beloved object at the center of the book, which is anything—which is everything— the talisman, the good luck charm, the thing you cannot live without yet live without. These are poems that ask the lasting questions: what to do with grief, brokenness, the ghosts that haunt our past and present lives? These poems provide no answers— only beauty, the perfectly conjured scene, each a small act of love that consoles and redeems.

—Angela Alaimo O'Donnell, author of *Andalusian Hours*

MERCER UNIVERSITY PRESS

Endowed by

TOM WATSON BROWN

and

THE WATSON-BROWN FOUNDATION, INC.

THE LOST THING

POEMS

Sarah Gordon

MERCER UNIVERSITY PRESS
Macon, Georgia

MUP/ P638

© 2022 by Mercer University Press
Published by Mercer University Press
1501 Mercer University Drive
Macon, Georgia 31207
All rights reserved

25 24 23 22 21   5 4 3 2 1

Books published by Mercer University Press are printed on acid-free paper
that meets the requirements of the American National Standard for
Information Sciences—Permanence of Paper for Printed Library Materials.

Printed and bound in the United States.

This book is set in Adobe Garamond Pro.

Cover/jacket design by Burt&Burt.

ISBN   978-0-88146-830-4
Cataloging-in-Publication Data is available from the Library of Congress

In loving memory of
Blanche Farley, a fine poet,
and
for Betty

Contents

Acknowledgments

"In the Valley of the Shadow" and "Acts of Love" *Shenandoah;*

"Creases, Folds" *Southeast Review;*

"Reliquary," "Acta Sanctorum," and "Vestige" *The Georgia Review;*

"Shades," "Threshold," and "Tactile Matters" *Sewanee Review;*

"A Call to Prophecy" *Confrontation;*

"How To Write a Memoir" *Arts and Letters;*

"Coverings," and "Spring," and a shorter version of "Mise en Scène" appeared in *Southern Poetry Review;*

"The Death of a Moth" and "A Dark and Feathered Thing" *Carolina Quarterly;*

"The Last American Tour, 1953" won Second Prize in the William Matthews Poetry Contest sponsored by the *Asheville Poetry Review*, which subsequently published the poem;

"Apertures: Andalusia" *Broad River Review;*

"It's felt like Sunday all day today," *Salt 2.*

The Lost Thing

"Everything had already happened. Hadn't it?"
Michael Ondaatje, *Warlight*

In the Valley of the Shadow

How she remembers, years after her mother died,
that big lake in her childhood, so wide, her father
announced solemnly, you couldn't see across.

How that first lesson in unfathomable distance
stayed with her, the limits of vision, the senseless
deep. Her toe could not touch bottom.

How she'd caught on to his little joke and made
of herself a containment vessel: settling heroically
behind the wheel, fingering the surgical stitches

as she awaited the doctor's call, breaking bread
with the enemy more than once, sifting through
the ashes. Hail Mary. Hell. Stepping up to the plate.

How now, in her old age, the ball of twine swiftly
rolls just out of reach. How the glass falls and breaks,
and water, so much water, twice or thrice

what the glass could hold, spills everywhere,
ruining page and paper and carpet and cloth.
How there is no such thing as graceful retrieval,

no such thing as unremarkable loss. Houses
empty like candy jars, scattering their treasures
on the lawn. The hole in the sofa is an open wound,

the dingy linen folded to hide the primal stains.
How cracked those cups that once ran over,
how seamed they are, those broken hearts, now

permanently out of stock, discontinued, like letters,
land lines, family. How memory exists without a sound track,
unvarnished scenes from a silent movie, rapid-fire,

endlessly tantalizing. How she clings to that intimate
cast of characters, fondly lingering over this one, that one,
making alterations, adding color, dialogue, markers, walls.

Exercises in Separation

Three times you make your way
to the teacher's desk, asking her again
to explain long division

and the mysterious practice
of borrowing numbers. Your friends,
heads down, are busy at it.

You learn: the knife peels back
the flesh in even the bodies
of class superlatives—

Cutest, Smartest, Most Likely To
Whatever. The ship sails, night falls,
the tide recedes. Candles burn.

Your clothes, flung across
the bedroom floor, blaze a trail
to you, fetal, bereft.

Below, laughter cracks the house
wide open. The others are doubled up,
doubled over. You parse the joke,

turning it back and forth,
inside and out, stupidly repeating
the punch line, lifting it to the light.

You later discover: A page has been torn
from your book, lifted by hands,
not yours, that do not wish you well.

Endings

In the 40s a kettle
was put on to boil
and we were told
to watch it. We kids
easily averted our gaze,
spinning the bottle,
turning the wheel,
guessing the number
of beans in a jar.
We tied the blindfold.
We hid in the woods
and ran home free.

But the pot steamed
and cracked, until
somebody took it
off the stove. Too late.
A fierce, beautiful
flower filled the Japanese
sky, its deadly bloom
the image on newsreels
everywhere. At our Saturday
matinee we squirmed,
sinking lower in our seats.

Hard to play well
with such light and heat
behind us, shoving us
ahead to God knew
what: walls falling,

streets buckling, flesh
too, peeling poison,
and nobody at home,
nobody anywhere.
No anywhere.

One evening as we walked
over to the Little Store
for an ice cream,
the sky fired up
Gold Ochre, Burnt Sienna,
and Venetian Red
brighter than we had ever seen
and more perilous.
Then it was, I remember,
that we scared ourselves
into life, our talk halting
but headed—for the first time—
toward fallout.

The Signs Followers

are only in West Virginia now, I hear,
but I could swear from time to time
I've seen one or two of them
lugging their unwieldy boxes
of rattlers and coppers into Walmart,
wedging their slippery treasure
into those steel carts, shoving
forward up and down the aisles.
In the hip pocket of one heavy
brother I glimpsed a strychnine
bottle; emerging from the other
pocket, a small, much-fingered Bible.
That day I tried to turn away
but couldn't help following him
up and down the aisles, at a distance,
me scanning soup cans and looking
heavenward if he chanced to turn
my way. He spent a good while
at frozen foods, spinach and the like,
leaning over the freezer, occasionally
shaking his head. He placed only
a few items into the cart, down beside
the big box. He was obviously
cautious or frugal or just unfamiliar
with how to do things. He wore boots,
a holey t-shirt, his Carhartts
slipping dangerously low in back,
and took his damned time. What
I wanted to see was what was in
that box, of course, what was so
valuable to him that he couldn't
even leave it in the truck or the trunk

of his car, what he couldn't let go of
even to do a little shopping.
Something he has that I want,
I admit, something he can't let go.
Or maybe that box is just a TV
he wants to return, one that, hell,
has to be programmed, or a mailbox,
or a microwave, some modern
miracle he won't enjoy.

Groundwork

In the seventies Elizabeth Bishop
called Lota her friend, not her lover,
a fable she liked to insert casually
into anecdotes and interviews,
under and over plot lines,
the perspicacious reporter:
My friend was at the market,
my friend was driving the car, not
my friend offered me her Brazilian home,
atop a treacherous but sublime
mountain, my friend was in fact
my lover and I, the jobless poet
taking my time and whatever else
I needed. Like a spoiled priest,
I expected my plate to be filled.
Cal Lowell, the madman,
offered marriage, I demurred,
never saying I already was.
Married, that is, or as much as,
to a life I couldn't name,
my torment a tangle like the jungle
below, the steep road to home
unmarked, perilous.
Then she died, and I drowned,
surrounded by my own reflection
everywhere back in Cambridge,
in small sycophantic circles,
critics scattered over my lines
like gardeners, digging context,
planting innuendo, watering
and watching the shy plant
emerge.

A Silly Thing, Broken

just after the package was opened,
a hasty move, regrettable, simply

embarrassing. You klutz, you think,
you're all thumbs! How could you?

What to do now with this imperfect
bowl, this chipped figure, this feeling,

where to place it or hide its small
scar, where shelve it, or for God's sake

toss it? Of little value, really,
not dear, a simple memento

that's likely lived a lot of life
but, still, neither momentous nor

beautiful, except perhaps to its owner,
who must have thought it so,

who may have wrapped it slowly,
with some patience, affection,

or may with hope have sealed the box,
gracefully twined the ribbon.

You or somebody like you
won't want to seem ungrateful.

The Acquisition of Knowledge

She hides outside her parents' door
to hear what they talk about
without her, away from her,
that kind of talk

She stands on tiptoe in the roses,
leaning away from the thorns,
to see through the window:
she's a camera into an empty room

She slides her fingers deep
into the crevasses of the couch,
discovers sullied tissues, brittle
somethings, pecan shells maybe,
they prick her fingers

She crawls beneath the bed,
she can just make it under,
she scrapes her arm, not badly,
she's barely breathing,
anonymous in the dark

She reaches to the top
of her father's high dresser
to steal some of his pocket change.
She pulls the forbidden novel
from her mother's shelf, sliding
the other books over to cover
the crime. She opens her brother's
underwear drawer to see
what's different. She sees,

and now she sees him,
sees another, the other,
him, them.

A Dark and Feathered Thing

"The maid was in the garden
Hanging out the clothes
When down came a blackbird
And snapped off her nose."

No ordinary days, none at all.
Mind your business, clear the deck,
fasten your britches, deposit
the check, gloat a while.
Watch out.

It can happen at a moment's notice
or no notice at all, the snapping
of the nose, the changing of the light,
the opening of the wound.

Even when you free your wits
to romp and cavort nearby,
those wayward kids start to yank
at your skirt, whining, slapping
each other playfully, then not so
playfully, milk on their mouths,
blood on their hands.

As you finally settle into
a fervent *delectatio morosa*,
pulling your hair, biting your lip,
staring at shapes the shadows
make, your wits wander away.
You last see them at the edge
of the wood, tossing rocks

at each another, though the next
thing you know they aren't
there, or anywhere.

There is only the fat blackbird
strutting onto the scene,
back and forth across
the page, bird tracks
leaving a splintery trail,
a hieroglyph, a riddle,
maybe a rhyme.

Creases, Folds

(The laundry, Good Shepherd Convent, Cork, Ireland)

The fallen girls of the Magdalene,
or derelicts as they were called,
scrubbing chalice veil and altar cloth,
once stood on tiptoe beside their mothers,
watching reverently as they stirred the pot,
sliced the bread, then, with heads bowed,
prayers said, dispensed the plates.
Soon the figure at the foot
of the bed, a fat dark-eyed queen,
will move closer, smearing blood all over
the sheets. Not the communion wine,
not the same, but soiled linen nonetheless,
to be washed, folded, stacked,
a chore hijacked by the extravagant
urge to shove to the front of the line
and out on the streets to find
what was taken, sold, passed
into other hands, like a birthright.
Or to follow the tangled path
to town where the wind shoves
the body down one street that runs
alongside another, intersected by yet
another—somebody's idea of order—
just the way the priest makes the sign
of the cross, drawing lines in the air,
walling in, walling out

Shades

The old aunts are still standing,
in turn, backs to the fireplace,
skirts lifted to warm their veiny legs.

Out on the front lawn, the crows
call to some distant power, planting
their crows' feet in the grassy

crows' paradise, green and wormy.
The father is a boy still, slinging
his rifle, a toy still, over his soft

shoulder and heading into the woods
where he'll remain for years on end,
forever seeking the slippery vagabondage

of freedom, fine fall afternoons
crisping into chill, the winter just ahead.
The mother is ever herself, at home

and alone, pots boiling over
but retrieved in time, her blue eyes
brimming a melancholy she can't serve up.

Just overhead in the dining room: clouds.
Just overheard, the old bickering,
with its raised brows, burning words.

Someone abruptly pushes back a chair,
rising from the table, a tearful ten
who won't forget, ever, her heart

carving a question mark
at the end of every breath.

Incarnadine

I can't rub the red out
or make it go away.
I step on it when I'm not
looking, I frame it
on the wall of my room.
I wear it, sing it, fall asleep
on top of it, wake
with it sanding the corners
of my eyes. I splash it
with cold water, roll
it under my arms, place
it under the tongue
in my cheek
until my face hurts.

Checking my image
in the mirror, I believe
I see a bindi, marking
the Third Eye, The Sixth
Chakra. But I am not
Hindu, nor, I confess,
do I plainly follow
the Christ whose hands
worked—and feet walked—
here, so they say,
bestowing people and place
with color, with matter,
with blood.

Painters take up
their brushes as if
all life depends on it,

and maybe it does.
I hold on to swaths
and snatches: in corners
of canvas, in that bright
ribbon binding the child's
braid, the one crimson leaf
defying the snow, the drops
on the carpet marking the trail
from the clearing to inside
the inside, to where it happened,
the scene of the crime.

When Van Gogh released the crows over that wheat field

the winds gathered. The ragged road ended in tall grass.
Those late strokes, that visual letting go, always stop us short,

invoke our chatter, our critical surmise. We continue to gaze
at the small canvas, the birds aloft, heading our way, the skies

ever dramatic in the Dutchman's dark eye. Even from cheap textbook
copies, the crows drop down among us, offering dejection, resurrection,

or just a sign of menace, according to those who know. Way back
in the '50s, we got an eyeful of the work, in Raleigh on our first trip

to a gallery. We were transfixed by the smeary colors, the ugly
self-portrait, but mostly the crows. In this art, nothing ethereal,

just plain people, wide brushes, stars like moons, a bandaged ear.
Meanwhile our lives spread out: Eisenhower, Korea, a white sports coat

and a pink carnation. And way over there somewhere, a quiet
increase in troops. We weren't looking, we didn't even have a map.

But always what is to come comes. Today we're told that the final
secret file on the young president's murder is soon to be released

on the cusp of some anniversary or other, we can't remember.
Even those of us who were alive then, who were in fact there,

shattered, our heels on the curb near the cortège or our arms
cradling a tree limb to see better the multitudes of mourners,

to stare down into the long dark limousine bearing the wife,
the small children: even we have smudged memories.

So let's return once more to the 35 millimeter film, his brain flying
loose, she, eternally desperate for retrieval, endlessly crawling over

the back of the car, an unseemly move in the relentless glare.
Fast forward, replay, replay. Not a cloud in the sky. A long time ago,

but not so long, we know. We are *fields of harvest wheat*. Auden wrote
what Van Gogh knew. I know he knew. Don't tell me

the painter didn't see it coming, the images in and out of control,
the crows just over his shoulder, thrumming, throbbing, close

The Lost Thing

innumeras errore vias
-Ovid

As you slide into
your old clothes,
put away your treasures
and turn,
you know suddenly
you don't have it.
Worse, you can't think
when last you did,
yesterday, the day before.
You accuse your fickle
eye, the way it meanders
in chapel from altar
to window to tree,
the flashy cardinal.
Doubt, that potent stain,
soils the fabric
of your memory.
You scour surfaces,
thrust your hand
to the back of the dream.
Down on your knees
you survey the underside
of things, their soft
beginnings, the dust.
You rummage
through the archives
of your ordinary life:
portraits of kin, nameless,
austere, scraps of paper,

broken vessels, covenants
kept, not, and something
else you don't want
anyone to see, for
the shape of this story
will be yours.
You gamely return
the way you came,
through the woods,
past the killing tree,
the cleft in the rock,
buried coin and empty
swing, every trace of play.
When the sun surrenders,
you're in the dark again,
spreading your one light
through the tall grass,
parting it with your fingers,
coming up empty-
handed, furious,
stumbling toward home.

Witness

"After such knowledge, what forgiveness?"
T. S. Eliot, *Gerontion*

Reliquary

We like to say,
Things gather dust, as though
with their substantial
power, things can summon
and corral, the way
young girls gather flowers
and sometimes young men,
or the way the king,
furious and aggrieved,
gathers troops at the border.
With her quick
fingers, the seamstress
gathers cloth into pleats,
and the old, shushing
the children, gather
thinlipped and self-
conscious at graveside
behind the little church
where many years ago
you folded me sweetly
into your arms,
in the hour just before
we packed the trunk
and stumbled down the path
toward sanctuary.
There we gently
unwrapped the heirlooms,
latching the cabinet
(it latched then),
to close off
the smell of cedar,
the head of St. Agnes

in its silver box, the splinter
from the cross that slivered
your thumb, drawing blood
and me to the scene
so that later, when
the children returned
we told the story, adding
the one about the lost sheep—
or was it the one
about the sheaves?

Witness

"The days that are still to come are the wisest witnesses."
—Pindar

1

When my brother set the woods on fire
my father asked me what I knew and when.
Then an earnest ten, I wanted to tell
the truth but never to put the ball in play,
never to ignite his ire against us all,
Mother, too. She'd begun to cry
and turned to gaze beyond the kitchen window
where the sheriff stood among scrub oaks and pines,
or what was left of them, our battlefield,
charred the way the movies taught us,
our forts, those mounds of rock and dirt, mowed
flat by the fire truck, nearly as broad as a tank.
So this is war, I thought, as I was ordered
to give away my general's boldest plan
(we have to smoke them out, he'd said)
and to betray my brother, whom I loved.

2

An eyewitness,
nodding in accord:
Aye, indeed I saw the man
slipping from the room,
he was clutching Gandhi's
glasses, which had lain
on the table, ready for
auction. I was witness
to that, aye, and to the lifting

of the plate, cup, and time-
piece, a still life nearby.
He dropped the relics
into a sack, so much
clanging treasure,
not much to show
for a life. They said
Gandhi would give away
his only spoon, his bowl.
He wanted nothing.
Sure, I know others claim
the spectacles with their round
gold frames belong to India,
a signal of her change of fortune,
her new way of seeing or being,
they say there was no theft,
only the sound of retreating
feet, unshod, rushing down
the stairs, out the door
into the street, lost
in dusty clouds of witness.

3

The paintings were stolen,
the library ransacked,
its puny monuments toppled,
broken heads rolled
across the marble floor,
the bard and his like.
In the garden more malice:
flowers jerked up,
their roots like wet hair
flung across the grass.

Yet it was the paintings
we mourned, as though
they were family,
as though perhaps
we'd created them
in another life, we knew
them so well: Cassatt,
Bellows, Hopper, O'Keeffe.
When we were girls
we'd walked among
them, threading our
way to French or math,
often, honestly, taking them
for granted, the way
a child assumes
endless childhood,
a bird, the branch.

And in a quiet
corner, we want to believe,
the wise old aunts
were watching
from their rockers
as, one after another,
the paintings were packed,
stacked, removed,
and they, humming
their lessons, urged
us not to count
on things, never to mind,
to remember
ars longa, vita brevis.

4

They asked me to explain
something I couldn't.
I couldn't say what it was
I saw except that I know
I saw it, sure as I live.
I could remember only
the teacher, bent and quiet,
tracing his lesson in the sand.
I would not tell them that.
Over again they sat me down
in the unforgiving light
and asked me to say
how I got to where I was
when I saw what I saw
and what it was I saw
just beyond the cave
where we'd lit the fire,
where we were hiding
with all we had,
our birthright
wound in soft cloth:
fractured delicate vessels
of ceremony and song,
crackling papyrus that told
our story in image and line,
idioms from another time
we hardly understood.

5

Butterfly and bougainvillea
and, just beyond,
the water buffalo
standing ankle-deep
in the stagnant pond
just before the building
at Phnom Penh
where the skulls
(some cracked
where the blow fell)
are lined up
row after row
as though they are
for sale. Instead,
they have to be dusted,
a joke that's wasted
on most visitors,
who want to look
and don't.
But they came to see.
The skulls are numbered
though they are not all,
say the counters,
who've been adding
and subtracting for years,
their totals up and down,
one million, three.
They say we'll never know
or want to know
the shadowy politics
of that day, the leaders
averting their eyes

as someone touched
a tender spot
and touched it again
and again
until the Khmer
with their knives
and ropes and blunt
instruments
caught fire.

Disclosures

Lescaux, France

Lamps then burned wood
from juniper trees, nestled
in stone bowls,
for day and night
the tunnels were dark
labyrinthine crawlspaces,
exercises in excavation
for the brave, perhaps
for those not afraid of falling
or of thin air, their limbs
akimbo, their bones
snapping, or perhaps
those just terrified
not to move. Sometimes
they must have writhed
forward with the ache of will,
making a way for the painters
who would come after,
who would balance
on their rickety scaffolds,
make their indelible marks,
creating, with a drop
of the wrist and a glance
overhead, immortal time,
the bison and horses plunging
over the rock, running free.
All of this hidden from us
for centuries, yet destined
to be unearthed, like those poems
in the trunk in Amherst,

or like that two-thousand-
year-old palm seed sprouting
from the ruins of Masada,
inevitable resurrections
defying prediction, prayer.
Need we, then, pointing
at the image, studying
the trope, stroking the
leaf, bother to name
the thing, to single it out,
that vital buried life
so like our own?

A Call to Prophecy

When he first knew something was wrong
he saw double out of his right eye,
and, tempted again and again to confirm it,
he kept moving his head in that direction,
a torturous pleasure, like tongue to gum
beneath the aching tooth.
Oh, he knew that something
was horribly amiss, everything twinned
as though shot through with some potent
fertility drug, landscape piled on landscape,
friends cloned on the periphery,
their narcissists' dreams come true.

Then he began to feel a slight pressure
near his left temporal lobe
as though a finger were insinuating itself
deep into his head and staying there.
Perhaps he'd been reading too much,
the brain irritably shaking off
all those words as one shakes out
a wet rag or a rainy umbrella at the door
or as one would like to slam
that door on all the uninvited guests
moving through his rooms, coughing,
laughing, telling their stale stories,
just asking for it, his sharp rebuke.

When first he stumbled, he thought little of it,
though his palms were raw from catching
his body on the pavement, raising himself
upright again, believing he'd tripped
on a shoelace, some threatening idea.

He looked to see if anybody saw.
No, but he was stiff for days afterward.
Unfolding himself on the soft couch,
he knew he needed to rise and walk
to prove that he could put one foot
in front of the other (that was all it was),
at least as far as the bend in the road.
Instead, he dreamed of the land,

a dry and compromised field
stretching into the horizon and planted
with plowshares and rusty engines,
tongued with green sprouts, thin
reminders of life next the cleavage
of earth, her wrinkled breasts,
her flaccid arms that will not hold
this metaphor, that will not hold
his dream, as he wakes into danger,
the sound of water running
water running somewhere

How To Write a Memoir

  1. Set the scene.

Inside the house, the sitting room that once
became the birthing room after it was
the courting room long before
it would contain the casket around which
are sitting kith and kin: the broken-hearted
Negro servant, the neglected middle child,
the father not as tall as we remembered,
the preacher imperfect with his presbyopian
eye and lurid tie standing next
the spoiled manchild the son and brother
who'll reap the inheritance, the youngest
girl squirming in her crinolines, pouting,
perhaps understanding a little
of the sounds of forced propriety
and simple grief, memory
you can always rearrange

  2. Create a cast of characters.

Who occupies center stage?
Is there any question? Time
for your performance, the tap
number you've struggled with,
a heel and a toe and a slap and a—
You feel bilious, you say billowy
when you call out to your mother
in the second row before
you lose it all: your dinner,
your new patent-leather shoes,
your pride. But do you want

to tell this? Why not the story
of being May Queen, the white
organza dress scratching your breasts,
your toes pinched, ankles weak
in high heels, the rest of you
decorated and shining
and nearly perfect but then
you ask What
does the May Queen do
what does she, can she, do
for her people who scurry around
her, her inferiors, of course, casting
resentful glances her way, picking up
the scraps, her train.
Play the headlines. Tell the story
of how the lecherous uncle leered
then teared when he was discovered
in *flagrante delicto*,
the one about the electrocuted aunt
whose face was seared a Halloween
horror, or the one about the bankrupt father
arriving home midmorning with the girl-
friend who was curious about
the house, the wife, what's tucked
away in dresser drawers.
Don't tell too much.

    3. Determine the shape of the plot.

Could be up—down—up
Or down down the lowest low
then up slightly a bit more.
There. A design on the chalk-
board, a series of candid shots,

or candied if you're addicted
to the happy ending
and not to the bittersweet one,
the one that resists resolution,
catharsis, that snags the heart
and pulls it up flailing,
gasping for air

The Last American Tour, 1953

The money she wired him
would be swallowed in drink,
she knew that, but wifely duty
or a perverse need to be right
made her wire it anyway
because she couldn't be there
to slap sense in him or pull his hair,
pound him on the back with her bare
fists, raging redfaced and grim.
But when they rang her in Swansea
to say he'd not waked up in the bed
at the Chelsea (19 whiskies, they said),
she screamed bloody murder
and got on a plane.
At St. Vincent's she bobbled
past reception: *Is the bloody man*
dead yet? Getting no answer
and no rise out of him,
she jumped him in the hospital bed,
pulled off by nurses who feared
he'd smother in the oxygen tent,
that plastic bag of breath
momentarily smashed flat—
the familiar stinky mouth
of her little fat man kept from her
at the last by what he needed to live
though he wouldn't and he didn't—
and she, fat too and alcoholic,
could have torn him limb
from limb. Instead, she cursed
John Brinnin, said she'd kill him,
but was seized and sent to detox,

while the comatose poet lay dying.
Days later, clean, still furious,
she packed all the beautiful shirts
he'd stolen so damned gleefully
from his foolish and generous hosts,
spat upon them, and snapped the bag shut.
And that's what we call closure.

Blind Man's Bluff

The soft cloth of the blindfold
tightens around your head,
pinning your ears. It smells
like the sweat of others.
You see nothing. You're asked
and then you tell them,
I see nothing, I feel nothing:
just what they expect
to hear. You're roughly turned
thrice, dizzied, set on your way,
some kind of aging wind-up toy.

The voices outside you
enjoin, beseech, commiserate,
dispensing the bromide
of functionary and counselor,
a dripping faucet you soon
won't hear in the tumult
and tears of visitation
where charity and common
sense slide on and off the tongue.
You're inconsolable.

Take the next step, you're told,
and so you lumber on,
arms outstretched, to touch
doors, trees, the people
in your path, that empty bed
wider than you'd imagined,
the closet you'd just as soon
lock, shutting in the life smells,

the textures and shapes
of memory's fierce embrace.

You've something in your hand,
something you're to take
somewhere and do something with.
One minute it's smooth, like cream
or cashmere, the next it's sharp,
a knife or a nerve. Though you'd like
to shake it, leave it behind,
you're stuck with it, that black hole
of endless absence.

It's felt like Sunday all day today

the old aunts say, lolling among the pillows on the porch.
Maybe it is, one says. I feel that way, too. Like you

I'm out of sync. Another straightens up, placing
her cup of tea on the table, as though to signal

a platitude emerging, at least some cautionary note,
from her ropey throat, bare now, unseemly. Sister,

what you got to say? a third commences. It's getting
on to suppertime. What shall we have to eat?

Maybe we'll treat ourselves to one of Mama's pies.
She won't mind. What day is it anyway? Any day

you want it to be, says the youngest. We're slap
out of time here. We're just old ghosts, you know,

hanging about this wide front porch, waiting
for the sun to set, the moon to rise.

Bounty

On the Sinking of the Lusitania, 1915

Off the coast near Kinsale, in Ireland,
the fishermen felt their nets fill
and suddenly spill over, the salmon
sliding and sloshing atop and under
one another by the bucketful,
the waves so brutal that the men
feared the end times, yet could not stop
clutching their bounty. They had not
heard the torpedo hit, did not suspect
the horror spawning this largesse.
Decades on, they said they should
have known: the sea's astonishing
upheaval, the rush of water over the hull,
that prodigious gift.

Just what did they tell their wives
when later that day they closed
their cottage doors and heard the news?
Soaked through, quietly triumphant,
did they dare to say, One man's misery,
et cetera, or even think that?
Hundreds of lives lost,
the liner resting at starboard
on the ocean floor, a monstrous
and immutable fact: Oh, not
easy, this telling, how the wind
and waves seemed to stop up
the men's ears as they clung
to their catch, smoke and flame
barely visible over their shoulders.   >

Anyway, they were looking the other way,
their silence as they worked the nets
broken by only an occasional oath,
a groan, an imprecation.

Tactile Matters

Roundness is all. Smooth surfaces,
the fat ball you wrap your hand around,

that sleeps in your open palm
until you decide what to do with it,

cars that curve and satisfy, low
to the ground, slick as river rocks

ahead on the road, which quietly
publishes its next move

so that you turn the vehicle
as you turn the page

or the potter's wheel, embracing
the wet clay, shaping it your way.

The wildhaired Einstein told us
how space is curved, like a canopy,

how the apple doesn't drop straight
down, but rather rolls down the slope

toward the spinning earth, a free
fall that takes our breath away.

What he didn't say was how
curves can please, how the whorl

of the shell and the full-term belly
mesmerize, how we trace the arc

with our fingers, to be a part of it,
as the soprano's voice follows

the golden stream easily upcurrent
and home again, resting in the sweet familiar,

while we, the clumsy, off-key children,
climb the sides of the ropey hammock,

giggling and trying to hold on,
to stay right-side-up,

the getting in and getting out
our scariest maneuvers.

The Old Way

Places there are in the Americas
where penitents fall to and walk on
their knees to the hallowed place,

places where those full of darkness
and remorse hoist a splintered cross
up and down main streets, sometimes

allowing themselves, later, to be nailed
to it in the city square. Places there
are in churches, stalls dark and private,

where the garrulous sinner whispers
through a grate, quietly, hoping
that collection of sentences will suffice,

where in the service itself the liturgy
enjoins us to bow and speak aloud
our failings in a rote and impersonal way.

Places where, as the poet noted,
prayer has been valid, where cracking
joints and failing bodies bend respectfully

onto bruising, unforgiving stone.
Places where, for hundreds and hundreds
of miles pilgrims, or so they call

themselves, stumble and rise
on their way to the shrine, hostelled
nights and missed directions adding

up to sacrifice, of a sort. Places
in the quiet corners of chapels
into which the adulterer slips

unnoticed, where the illegal
and the illegitimate exchange
glances and sink into shadow.

On even the most carefree day
places there are in the chambers
of the heart where the penitent

finds herself in painful
and chastening recollection,
seeking shelter and the old way,
the path or the place
or the moment of surrender.

Apertures: Andalusia

For Flannery O'Connor

Each day the eye finds fresh fare,
filling the homely bowl
of routine with slivers of light
and shade so that even the cracks
in the plaster are crooked roads
to somewhere:
A car shudders up
the dusty drive, cadenced
voices pass the time of day
in the familiar dance,
gauging their moves, a bow,
a do-si-do around the corners
of the room, as glasses perspire
onto the tabletop, a door shuts.
A boy or a man or just a figure
in the distance climbs
onto the sloping back
of a mule. Somebody brings
news that won't wait the telling,
that doesn't bear repeating
but will be repeated,
somebody's mouth a long O,
agape, *agape*, a love feast.
The bloody sun burns low
enough to set the woods on fire,
one arm grazes another
that doesn't want to be touched.
A plate of slightly rotting fruit
rests on the dining room table,
ink-smeared fingers endlessly

turn the pages of the newspaper
or carefully place the rosary
in the bureau drawer.
A former tenant visits,
he doesn't want to leave,
he stands for a long time
in the middle of the yard
running his fingers through
his greasy hair, clearing
his throat, repeating himself.
The tops of trees are silvered
by an antique light.
For a moment a peafowl
stands on one leg
on the roof of the barn,
a live weather vane,
another fans himself
in the front yard.
Nobody notices.
A window slams shut.
The hired man's children
in the back of the car
swat each other with comic books.
Is that smoke on the horizon,
do you smell it, no, well then.
A meal is served, nobody speaks.
Outside, it's early evening,
the bats lilt through the air
as though they are beautiful.
They are small black doors ·
into the dark.

Unraveling

In the spread that thread
you pulled, no end to it, all string
soon enough. You might break it
between your teeth or cut it.
Still it will find itself again
and snag, and you will pull it.
You won't want to,
but you will.

Acts of Love

*He showed me a little thing, about the size of a hazelnut,
in the palm of my hand, and it was as round as a ball. I
looked at it and thought,—What can this be? And the
answer was generally thus:—It is all that is made.*

Julian of Norwich, *The Cloud of Witnesses*

Acta Sanctorum

Ever notice that some machines, after you've shut them off,
keep humming for a while, whether you're listening or not?
So it is with the saints. They, being dead, yet speak.

Lord knows we all search for a way to be, a fire
to sit around, some sign at the intersection of major
highways. Saints, too, with their guileless gaze,

must look for the place where purpose stands up
and steps closer, where the full wrinkled robe
of the body, now graceful, goes it alone.

Benedict saw the whole world in a sunbeam,
and when wild Augustine let his finger fall
on the sacred text, all was changed.

Aldhelm danced like a clown in the public square,
to win hearts, then souls, he said, and we love him
for that impish joy, that easy surrender

of the propriety or sobriety that makes some
hate the faith. His life hums away, a happy tune.
And why not? Need saintly lips be pursed and grim?

Oh martyrdom's another matter!
When we let slip that armload of belongings
and the most loved bowl shatters at our feet, perhaps

then, of all times, we hold our bodies close. The martyrs,
standing in their corner, do not invite our company,
they possess only readiness, which is, of course, all.   >

Their clothes are deeply soiled and won't come clean.
We don't pretend to see as they did, those much older
siblings. They'd already left home before we were born.

On Placing a Big Thing into a Small Space

like a ship in a bottle,
ten buffoons into the clown car,
the vast landscape into the photo,
this complaint into words on a page.

Your visits home, long ago:
you remove much of what is you,
peeling off one layer after the other,
thinking of the words *acclimate*
and *tedium* and *angst*
(it's always about words with you),
filling your seat at the table,
ready to talk about the world
as it's seen from there.
No one asks a question of you,
no one seems to want to know—
your work, your poems, your lover,
the chance for expression, confession,
suitcased and closed.

You sleep on the edge of a child's bed,
hiding yourself from yourself to appear
familiar in the mirror provided.
But you won't hold your breath for long.
You are intact and they, none the wiser.
You drive south the next week, alone
beside those frozen Carolina fields,
the sun in your eyes. You're unshriven,
relieved, reassembling your life.

Coverings

I love the skin you're in,
I tell the chameleon,
who flashes me a sidelong
glance from his leafy chaise,
lounging green on green,
his throat throbbing coral.
I'm envious, too, of the polar bear
whose black flesh, a trade secret,
lies beneath that glacial fur—
one with the cold,
his underwear invisible.
Were it not for the light
the indigo bunting
would be in funereal crepe
and not a sight to see.
Thus I give thanks
for the light and,
come to think of it,
for indigo, even for its tortured
history, which gives us indikon,
aniline, a plant, a shade, a fiber,
a thread of lapis in a mummy
wrap, Persian rugs,
the blue flags of empire,
the dye in our britches
that matches your eyes,
which lead me to disclose
this, just this much,
and no more.

Paradise Garden: Howard Finster

When he was sixty, the smeared face
on his thumb he knew to be
the call of the Lord, who asked
him to put the colorful fragments
of the world fallen at his feet
back together again, to reassemble
assembly, to paint what's lit up
or light up what's not, dropping
brushes into vats of color, pools
of image—jasper, onyx, cerulean,
the bloodiest rose, shards of shell,
shellac, undiluted Elvis, blanched
and blessèd Jesus, elephants, angels,
tall wobbly churches—impaling nailing
crucifying trees and branches.
Every time he hit a board
with that nail a wound
the size of a mouth or a heart
opened inside him and the Word
came to cauterize it, searing
and sealing the act, by which
he beguiled his audience, rebuilt
Eden, justified and sanctified
that little corner of north Georgia,
where folks take things literally.
I mean everything.

Mise en scène

Sometimes Stieglitz set up
his camera on the street
or in a park and let whoever
walked into it walk into it
or whatever happened
happen. He must have been
drawn to the quotidian
or possessed a simple desire
for the haphazard, a leaf
or two scuttling by,
a couple bickering
with malicious zeal,
strolling pigeons inspecting
trash, and the accidents of rain
and weather.

You see where this is headed.
Scenes are set, doors are open,
and gardens look green, inviting,
so we walk onto them, through
them, into them. Take that un-
documented migrant in Paris
the other day. He saw the child
dangling like a doll from the balcony,
so many floors up, and simply began
to climb, his silhouette on the wall
a fly on the camera's eye.
That's what we call exposure:
an impulse, a shout, an urge to help,
a rushing forward into the light
and danger, danger everywhere.

Ballast

To gain altitude, to be
most perfectly ourselves
in the basket of our conveyance,
we first tossed our clothes,
watched them slide down the air.

Our balloon, the *Gazelle*, sewn
from silk dresses of the generous
belles of Richmond (their boldly
sacrificial gift), wafted brightly
in palest light over the enemy line.

Once we found equilibrium,
we used our rudders to dig
through the currents, marking
the Union boys' approach
just as they marked ours

from the *Intrepid*, a few miles
away on the river's other side.
And what was this languid lookout
but the power the land and family
held over us, her fields stretching

beneath and beyond
our considerable height and color.
Had we managed reliable steering
and a sufficient sense of irony
we might have exchanged

greetings, admired the others'
ingenuity, looked each other
in the eye. But as things stood
we could say only, We must lose
something, maybe everything

that's ballast: our rage, our pride,
the celebratory bottle of wine, those long
and useless Sunday afternoons, all our excuses,
discourse, argument, casuistry,
even the green jacket with the golden thread.

We must find our way up and away
from the skirmishes, the blood,
and the looking. Lord, we have looked
too long, our eyes burn with the looking
and the seeing, the opening and the closing,
the black-and-white, the color,
the storage, the steerage.

On the Death of a Moth

"He was little or nothing but life." Virginia Woolf

Floating on the coffee
near the bottom of the cup,
you are an airplane
stalled on a shallow sea,
flotsam or jetsam, whatever.
Perhaps your antennae,
those frail coordinates,
or your filament legs
betrayed you this time,
I think, as I spoon you
from your dark pond.
Or perhaps you simply
floated down for a closer
look, seeing something
you couldn't live without
or live without knowing,
and lost your balance
on the rim. Or were you
merely escaping turbulence,
a fusillade of gnats,
the traveler's baffling malaise?

Your tweedy self
won't be much mourned,
I know, in the frenetic
and inevitable yielding
of small things: birds
numbskulling into glass,
squirrels flat and still
on the median, roaches' legs

treading the air,
but when your left wing
suddenly shudders—as though
with a small electric charge—
I look again and then again,
hopeful that the breeze
of my breath threads us together
(*spero, spiro, spiramus*),
that we will die another day.

Threshold

The open door beckons
a way out or a way in

when all else seems
narrowly walled and white

The open door is a frame
for a painting, precisely

measured, carefully cut,
handmade, man-made

with power to close off
as a rope or an eye cordons

off or includes everything
pertinent to the scene

A clean aesthetic, simply
offering what it offers

seeing what it sees
and allows you to see

the river, the road,
the long line of trees

behind which the soldiers
stare, then languish

You see them there
their arms weary with

holding the guns
withholding their fire

You see them in the light
and think of them

at night, your soft gown
blowing against you

as you sketch yourself
into Life, entering

its scarred and beautiful body
its wide and open eye.

Vestige

in memoriam, Harry Crews, 1935–2012

No accounting for it.
Just debris scuttling across fields
toward town, mud tracked
across a fine carpet, as
that sorry Abner Snopes,
pinched lip, plugged cheek,
face as lined as a map
and as hard to read,
pounds on the front door
of the big house and refuses
to wipe his feet.

Sarty and the other boys
mimic his mood until, late
in the scene, come the fire,
the gospel singer, the gator wrestler,
the misfits, the misaligned,
and that kid who catapulted
into the boiling brine, meeting
the swine flesh to flesh, his skin
later peeling off like pages
of a tablet or scraps of cloth
our mama could make a quilt of,
I reckon, and throw out on the line

In the Elysian Lounge

Beyond the western ocean at the end of the earth,
behind the veil of sunset, he and she and you
and I and everybody we've ever known or
believed we knew or even wanted to know

will call each other by name and sit down
together to share lifetimes and love lines,
all of the misery and joy that underscores
the quotidian. We'll be still, attentive,

at ease in our fleshless selves, asking
and telling, spinning at will in and out
of time and the stunning wonder of our days,
admitting the schemes we used to hold life fast:

those walls we built, the corners we cut,
the hurt feelings, the blind eye and callous word.
In the evening quiet, lulled by the great sigh
of the sea, we'll be in the presence of those

we've loved well—or poorly—even the ones
we fought until blood came. But, hey, not
for Judgment! No. Not the gods' squinting,
assessing eye, not a wrenching asunder,

neither shame nor regret. No pariah, scapegoat,
martyr. No side to choose. It's been chosen.
No red line in the sand, so long ago stained.
In the Elysian Lounge with its sweeping view,

blessèd draughts of purest air, we'll gain
only perspective, only the eternal life that our stories—
told in the way we alone can tell them—will give.
We'll be leaning close to hear. And that's all.

The God of Everything

asks what you think you know
of this earth, her steeps and scarps,
her invisible corners, hiding places,
holy places, sacred waters,
her children rummaging through
garbage at the edge of the camp,
the cities you'll never set foot in.
Seas with their fill of waste,
dangerous and indestructible,
troops staring into bright death
and moving toward it, slaves
knee-deep in the swamp, ships
with places to go, assignations
you'll never be asked to keep.
A mother sheltering an umpteenth
child against the blistering wind,
a large plane scrolling toward
a crash, firelanes, fireflies,
languages you won't learn
or be expected to learn,
acronyms, megabytes, torts,
legal precedent, minus numbers,
real revolution with banners
and blood. Abdication, curses,
illegitimate this and that,
rites of succession, possession,
the pusillanimous guarding
of the hoard, pimps, protégées,
books of fine print and power
you manage not to read,
coffins lowered, ashes boxed,
boxcars callously loaded with aliens

clacking toward encampment
and slow death, the conveniently
averted eye. The tearing of the hymen,
the ripping of the shroud, forgiveness,
absolution, the reconciliation
of opposites, of enemies, of colors,
of sexes in one body, the body
engendered or not, tipped
one way, another, transported,
if you will, to safety

Miracle

"Did Lazarus die a second time?"
—H. Laxness, *Independent People*

Somebody peeled away
the shroud and saw
fingers trying to feel,
eyes opening against
their will, the man's body

indistinct, one dimensioned,
a negative coming into light,
slowly enfleshed.
He was dead everybody said,
we were sure of it,

yet we gave him water
and bread, bathed his face
and hands, blessing him
as we would bless a child
summoned from fretful sleep.

As everybody closed in
to touch his flesh, soon again
moist and lively, he seemed
more dazed than pleased,
our questions clotting the air.

His breath caught, he stuttered,
he could not tell us, could not
or would not. Someone asked
his sisters about the smell,
that carnal festering mingled

with pungent burial spices,
how to get rid of it.
Time, in time, they shrugged,
fearing their rejuvenated brother
would never live this down,

would ever be pointed to,
pointed out, portrayed
and written about,
his days returned to him,
so much pocket change.

So, after the rending of garments,
the keening, the setting sun
and the quickening,
he stumbled home
to take up where he left off,
endlessly indebted,
no choice in the matter.

Spring

Now let's hear it for the eye,
the gluttonous, lively eye,
its rootedness, its fine fibers,
from the cornea's bay window
through the vitreous humor
to that electric thread
nestled in the dark inner wall
where millions of retinal rods
and cones, stacked in a crowded
closet, wait to be touched.

The eye eats the scene:
branches beaded in light,
the insistent greens, the golden
dust at the heart of the bloom,
all lines—straight, bent,
broken—even that distant
stirring that may be life
or nothing at all.

The eye is a circus trick,
the clown's gift of the bucket
with no bottom that holds
everything, your mother's seamed
brow as she leans over the fence
to inspect the havoc the deer
have wrought, the garden despoiled,
the redtailed hawk snatching
the wren, the spider's single

subtle thread, and your lover
in profile, considering, you imagine,
you and the mortal indulgence
of spring.

Acts of Love

She approached the painting
reverently, as had many another,
and when she stood before its large white
center inside the large white edge,
she kissed it, a chaste closed-mouth
kewpie-doll smack of Sunlit Bronze
changing it forever,
or so the restorers concluded
when they could not remove
the lipsticked shape.
An act of love, she said.

How not to understand
that impulse, the simple desire
to claim and connect,
imprint or, for that matter,
be imprinted, to welcome
the stinging, needling tattoo?
Don't skies beg to be clouded,
water to be stirred?
My sweet friend Laurie, dead now
these many years, declared at thirty
she wanted crowsfeet
to inscribe her aging skin,
an outward and visible sign
of her grand embrace of life.

Why does the cat leap
onto the middle
of taut, fresh sheets?
What makes the generals
stride onto the desert,

scoring the pristine sand?
Why is passion colored purple?
And flaunted?
Does the forehead ask
to be blessed, the back
to be lashed?
Nature abhors a vacuum
or adores it.
In the margins
of all my childhood books,
I scrawled my name.

About the Author

Sarah Gordon, Professor Emerita at Georgia College in Milledgeville, is a widely published and award-winning poet, with work appearing in *Christianity and Literature*, *Sewanee Review*, *Georgia Review*, *Shenandoah*, *Confrontation*, *Southern Poetry Review*, and elsewhere. She is the author of an earlier poetry collection, *Distances*, as well as *Flannery O'Connor: The Obedient Imagination* and *A Literary Guide to Flannery O'Connor's Georgia*. A recipient of The Governor's Award in the Humanities, Gordon lives in Athens, Georgia.